Spirituality
in
Daily Life

A BK Publications Book

First Publication 2000

ISBN 1-886872-18-X

Published by the Brahma Kumaris Information Services, Ltd. Global Co-operation House, 65 Pound Lane, London NW10 2HH, UK

Printed by Leighton Printing, London, UK

Contents

What is Spirituality?

WHAT IS SPIRITUALITY?

Spirituality is not the same as religion. There can be religion without spirituality, and spirituality can bring a sense of sacredness that is common to many religions and yet need not be expressed through any of them. But to many people the word 'religion' has become merely a label, referring to a ritual or fundamentalism with little or no spirituality. Yet the root meaning of religion is 'to join together or to re-connect' suggesting a re-uniting of the self with its Source. And that is very spiritual, in fact it is the very purpose of spirituality.

Spirituality begins with understanding. Sometimes it may seem to come suddenly and sometimes it comes only gradually, but it does come and it deepens within me to the degree that I apply what I understand in my life. The three most important concepts that form the basis of spiritual understanding are:

1. the understanding of myself and how I view myself in relation to the world.

2. the understanding of the Source or Supreme and my relationship with Him.

3. the understanding of the law of cause and effect, or 'karma'.

Spirituality can never be disassociated from way of life. Spirituality is that non–material energy which actually empowers and governs my life and my every action. If I think that I have to leave the world or go and sit on a mountain top or merely subscribe to a set of religious beliefs in order to 'be spiritual', then there is something missing within my understanding of what spirituality means.

Just as there are laws that govern matter, so there are also spiritual laws. The law of karma, the spiritual law of cause and effect, informs me of my own responsibility regarding how I behave and the consequence of my actions. The understanding of the soul and the Supreme are also highly relevant and applicable to my life. In the theory and model of reality taught by the Brahma Kumaris, there is wonderful, intricate knowledge that can be studied and experimented practically. In the following pages we will look at the most important aspects of this knowledge.

Knowing Myself

KNOWING MYSELF

The first step in spirituality is to know myself. The ordinary way of thinking of myself is in terms of gender, age, race, profession, relationships and so on. Instead of this ordinary way, let me see myself as spiritual. Let me see myself as an eternal being, a powerful energy encapsulated in an infinitesimally small point of light. With this shift in consciousness I can become liberated from all sorts of limitations and chains that affect most people's lives. For example I may be in the role of mother or teacher or I may be someone who possesses a fine car. None of these things is bad in themselves, but if my happiness, sense of identity or security depends on any of these, to that extent I am controlled by them and not the master of my own mind.

When I see myself as not just a body but as an eternal spirit, I am liberated from much fear, because the greatest fear we have is the fear of death. When I accept that this body is just temporary, whereas I am eternal, there is no more fear of the death of the body.

I know that at some point I will leave this body. But this is no cause for unhappiness or fear when I have the understanding that there is another human body, another experience waiting for me. With this understanding I can let go of the attachment and possessiveness I have when I identify with my body. There is such a sense of freedom in going beyond the fear and limitations connected with the body. My attitude changes because I am secure in my own eternal being.

If I have only one set of clothes to wear I am very possessive and attached to it because I have only the one, but if I open my wardrobe and have many more then I am not so attached to or dependent on the set of clothes I am wearing! In the same way, although the body is far more valuable than clothing, the body is not my source of life and security; it is not me.

The body is like my car; I keep it clean and well-maintained but I, the driver, never think I am my car! Being just a body instead of being the body means that although there is the responsibility of looking after it, because it is through the body that I perform my daily actions, and interact with people and the world, there is no fear of losing it. So one very important aspect of knowing myself is that I am eternal. Another very important concept is self-respect. Self-respect is absolutely essential in order to remain stable in this awareness of who I am.

Self-respect

SELF-RESPECT

Self-respect is valueing my own existence.
When I value myself I will also have respect
for others around me and for all life. When
I have self-respect I can remain stable
internally, with no misplaced sense of either
superiority or inferiority. It is only when I
lack self-respect that I am dependent on
others to support me to give me
confidence. When I value myself I will also
be able to have respect for others around me
and for all life. I am able to give myself
space and give others space too. The
liberating state of 'no expectations' comes
when I accept and respect myself. I am able
to 'let go' and I don't make demands on
others. Others don't have to do as I ask or
fulfil my desires. I am free and can help
others to become free. When I have self-
respect it is easy to have respect for others.
Many values are missing in the world today,

but I would suggest that the main missing value is respect. My parents never had to tell us to respect them, and 40 years ago it was natural to respect your parents. Today I don't think that is generally the case and parents themselves often become resigned to the lack of respect from their children. But in accepting such a situation perhaps they forget that it is in the atmosphere of the home that values are learned through example.

There are of course cases where parents stay together and children see respectful relations between them and in the extended family. However, where parents do not stay together, loyalties can easily get divided and confused, leading to a dilution of respect. This is not to point a finger of blame at anyone, but rather see what realistically has happened to the world and how fragmented everything has become. When children grow up in an environment of respect for others and the self, they will have a strong foundation for building respectful relationships in later life.

Discrimination

DISCRIMINATION

Lack of respect has a very interesting impact on the global situation. Discrimination is an example of this. Within countries and between countries, no place is free from it. Depending on the minority groups or the historical situation, the target becomes different but the seed, the root, is the same: lack of respect for human life, and lack of dignity within the self. Without a feeling of one's own dignity, how can one recognise the dignity of other human beings?

If we want to have a world where human rights and dignity prevail, where there is respect amongst people, the starting point has to be within the individual. I have to start by seeing myself as a spiritual being, the inner self, because if I place value on the colour of my hair, skin, accent, occupation or any of these external things, then naturally I will judge and compare others according to these criteria.

"People with light hair are very good but anyone with red hair has a temper and may cause me problems. "An example like this may seem laughable but is not so dissimilar from the criteria we generally and probably subconsciously use to judge others. We forget how easy it is to let external things influence our consciousness and we react spontaneously without even realising we are being influenced. Someone has a pretty face and we feel she must be a nice person. Someone is 'like me' in some way so, on that basis, I assume he is OK.

Concept of the Self

CONCEPT OF THE SELF

When I see myself as a spiritual being, the shining point of light within the body, there are no limits, no bondages, no problems.

There is no question of being better than the next person, because when I value myself as a spiritual being I automatically value others in the same way. They too are shining points of light within their bodies, they are all my spiritual family. In this state I value myself but there is no arrogance or ego. Awareness of my true inner self and respect for others move absolutely in parallel together.

It is when these two are lacking that discrimination arises.

Respect for the Environment

RESPECT FOR THE ENVIRONMENT

Another global problem which has arisen from our lack of self understanding and self respect is that of the environment. Why is it that we have exploited and damaged the planet, our home in which we all live? The answer can be traced back to a lack of respect for life on all its forms. However many charters may be signed and environmental laws passed, we will continue to damage the environment and destroy our home until we learn to respect life and I can only respect life 'out there' when I respect myself 'in here'. I recognise the world 'out there' as the vast, wonderful theatrical stage onto which I come to play my part with others. It is only where spirituality has been divorced from our practical lives that we have severe problems. Spirituality is not a luxury, something for people who have nothing else to do but sit around and meditate! In fact, it is the lack of spirituality in daily life that is causing the breakdown and destruction of our planet and our civilisation.

As we restore spirituality we can find methods of working together to create better selves and a better world. Thus we can see, looking at our global relationships, that spirituality is an integral part of life.

We need to remind ourselves constantly that spiritual consciousness or spiritual awareness means first and foremost to see and experience myself as a spiritual entity. This is the only secure basis for true self-respect and respect for others. In this awareness I see others as beings of light like myself. I do not put up walls or barriers in communication. I am able to value others because I am secure in myself. I am able to respect all life. I am able to work in harmony with the world around me and am not compelled to exploit or dominate it in any way. All this is based on just this first step of spiritual awareness. I apply it in my life and make effort to maintain the consciousness of who I am in my vision and in all my relationships, including my relationship with nature.

So how do I maintain this consciousness in my daily life?

Maintaining Spiritual Awareness

Maintaining Spiritual Awareness

How does a child know who he or she is? When a child takes birth, it doesn't know its name, its parents, the situation into which it has been born or what to expect. It is born totally innocent. Then it is given information, which it gradually imbibes and uses to form a concept of itself and its relationship to others. Unfortunately the information that is being fed to us all from birth onward mostly draws our attention to what is external and physical. This gets recorded deeply within us.

Being aware of spirituality and imbibing spiritual information work in the same way. The difference is that this process is not normally reinforced externally.

The child is exposed to the mother, father and

family, and later peers and 'society'. They will all feed it and reinforce it with the same information which unfortunately is contrary to the spiritual reality. Wherever I go, whatever I do, people respond to me as a body, people look at me as a body. People will work with me in terms of my role, gender and so on, and not with any spiritual vision. Therefore it is I, and I alone, who must constantly work this out for myself and take the responsibility to remind myself who I am, as I continue to deal with life situations.

I need to let my inner awareness filter all that comes from the outside and constantly remind myself of the spiritual truth that I am the soul. This is where the challenge of spirituality comes. Without this active effort of imbibing spiritual awareness and applying it, everything is just being passively absorbed.

Whatever is coming to me most of the time is

from the outside and is, in fact, negating reality, so I have to respond to this situation myself. The first counter measure is meditation.

Meditation

MEDITATION

Raja Yoga is the name given to the type of meditation and study practised by the Brahma Kumaris. Literally, 'raja' means 'king' and 'yoga' means 'link' or 'connection', implying the highest link, or the connection which will make me a king, or ruler over myself. There are limitless creative ways to go into meditation using thoughts based on Raja Yoga philosophy.

We do not use any special posture or breathing techniques and we usually meditate with the eyes open. The reason for this is to train myself to be able to find my inner reality quickly wherever I am and not be dependent on any special conditions. The essence of the technique is that I sit quietly, withdraw my thoughts from the body and focus on that tiny point of light behind the centre of the forehead. All experiences of meditation flow from this consciousness. All time spent in meditation is valuable but the most important time is first thing in the morning because this creates the right perspective for the rest of the day.

If I don't start the day in this way then the influences throughout the day tend to be so strong that it becomes very easy to forget who I am. When we forget who we really are, it is like having spiritual amnesia where everything gets out of focus and we begin to think in the ordinary way again, seeing ourselves as body, gender, profession and so on. When I spend time in the morning every day being aware of who I am, this allows my own self-esteem, my own self-respect, to re-emerge.

Study

STUDY

The next step, following the sequence of the day, is to expose myself to spiritual knowledge. Spiritual knowledge feeds my meditation and the more spiritual knowledge I have, the better equipped I am to face the world and deal with any situation that comes up.

Knowledge and power are closely related to each other. Depriving someone of information or knowledge, dis-empowers them. The converse is also true. The more knowledge one has, the greater the possibility of self empowerment. So, we begin each day with silent meditation, followed by time spent in spiritual study.

It is possible to study alone anywhere but the company of other spiritual students generates a powerful and positive atmosphere, so it is a great advantage to be able to come together with a group of like-minded people and study together. Regular study in such a gathering is a tremendous source of strength. In over 4,000 centres world-wide, students of Raja Yoga gather together daily in this way before they go off to work.

Two additional practices can also be of enormous help.

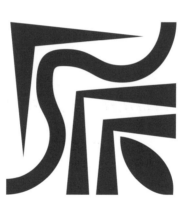

Traffic Control

TRAFFIC CONTROL

The first practice is to stop what I am doing every so often for what we describe as 'traffic control', i.e. halting the non-stop thought traffic of the mind.

Whilst I am at work or doing other things, I pause for just a few moments to rest and refresh the mind - perhaps every hour on the hour for three minutes, perhaps every two hours, whatever is convenient.

By creating these 'traffic control' times I can experience that inner space to remind myself who I am, and to check my attitude in what I am thinking and doing.

A New Vision of Others

A NEW VISION OF OTHERS

The other simple practice I can develop is
that of looking at others in a new way. To
look at each one as a body with certain
physical characteristics brings many
distractions to the mind. There is distraction
not only in the variety of physical
characteristics but also in people's mood
changes, which we in turn react to. For
example, I may be feeling stable and at ease
but then I see a face looking irritable or
angry and this suddenly causes my mood to
drop. Or a person may simply walk into the
room with very noticeable clothes and I am
pulled into a whole new train of thought
about what they are wearing and why.

Physical differences, facial features and others'
moods all have an impact on me. I need a very
powerful method to maintain my own inner
stability and a state of love, peace and joy.

One method to protect me from being distracted is to look at the forehead of each individual and 'see' him or her as a spiritual entity – as a tiny point of light. This reminds me to relate to others on the deeper level of who we really are. I won't be distracted and my own state of mind will remain stable.

Interestingly, as this method is developed, I become more sensitive and aware of the spiritual individuality and needs of others. But the main result for me is that I remain stable and my relationships also have the possibility of remaining stable. It is because of the ordinary 'body conscious' vision we have of others, i.e. a vision based on consciousness of the body that so many problems arise in relationships.

The Importance of Relationships

THE IMPORTANCE
OF RELATIONSHIPS

The next aspect of spirituality is my relationship with the Supreme or God and exploring how that influences me. It is relationships that have the greatest impact on us, and deeper the relationship I have with someone, the greater the impact that person will have on my life. For example, even if I go away on holiday with someone, I will often come back using words and expressions and even mannerisms which that person uses. This is on an external level. On an internal level they will have influenced me even more. All relationships have their impact.

Generally, we have not allowed ourselves to be influenced by God in this way. Usually this is partly because we are afraid to allow this to happen and partly because we don't know exactly who God is. We don't know how to go about setting up a connection with this Being and so we don't consciously spend time in His company.

Discovering God

DISCOVERING GOD

I know a woman in her eighties who although she had always believed in God and felt His presence in her life, found that when she came into the knowledge of Raja Yoga late in her life this relationship changed. She described it in this way. For her it was as if she had been in correspondence with a pen friend for many, many years and finally had met that pen friend face to face. What she found was that in certain aspects the image she had had was confirmed but in other aspects, where she had assumed and expected certain things, she discovered something quite new and different.

This is the experience of many people. Others have had no interest in God or are even against the whole notion of God before they discover this relationship.

Many of us have had some feelings or thoughts

about a Supreme Being but have not had a precise, specific method of being able to connect with Him and develop that relationship. We question where we can find information about exactly who this One is, where He is and how we can make contact. The awareness of myself as a soul is the first step in practising the easy natural method of connection with God, which we call Raja Yoga. The second is to understand God, the Supreme Soul as a Being of Light. Then, within a moment, with just one thought, I can make that connection.

When I suddenly find the key to contact someone easily having previously experienced difficulty or uncertainty, in this regard the quality of the relationship will naturally change. I begin to really feel God's presence in my meditation. As I continue to maintain this connection I will begin to be influenced by

God's qualities, love, purity, joy and peace. These qualities will be awakened and empowered in me and this in turn will influence my life and actions. The company we keep is such a powerful influence on our lives and characters. We naturally tend to avoid spending time in the company of a discontented person because their company is uncomfortable and leaves us with a similar feeling. By contrast, we will seek out the company of someone who is happy and contented and loves us. God is the most contented of all souls and the most loving. By allowing God to come into my life and influence me, I too will become contented. The quality of my relationships with others will also change. These are immediate and long-lasting benefits of knowing God.

Contract with God

CONTRACT WITH GOD

In all close relationships there is always some kind of understanding or 'contract', whether written or unwritten, formal or informal. When God comes into my life, what are the 'terms' of my relationship with Him? There are so many aspects to our relationship with God. He is my Father, Mother, Teacher, Guide, Friend and Companion. In fact, God is beyond gender and although we usually refer to Him as 'He' this is largely because of the constraints of language; God is my Mother just as much as Father, but whatever the relationship may be, I need to understand what it is that I can receive and what I have to observe or give.

In any relationship of love, I won't ask myself what I have to give but will instead ask the other person what he or she would like. If I were going to cook a meal, I would first ask my partner to say what he or she would like to eat rather than just thinking of what I want to cook. I would be happy for the other person to make the choice and would adjust and accommodate accordingly. The more love there is, the more I am willing to adjust. If there is no love, then instead of wanting to give I just make demands about what I want. This kind of situation is worth looking at more closely because although I may say my behaviour is based on love, is it really? It is important to examine our relationships and think about this. If it is just my needs or desires that I am concerned with then I must question the quality of my love.

This is how we might look at the give and take or exchange in close human relationships. The same applies in the context of my relationship with the Supreme Soul, except that the Supreme Soul, God, is really quite demanding!

I could take notice of my own and everyone else's desires, and let those be the basis of my actions, but God wants me to ask my heart what I think He would like me to do. For example, before I speak to others, let me speak to God in my heart and ask Him what He wants me to say or do.

When I open my heart and lay claim to His love and peace I am able to give love and peace in return. This is all He wants from us and it is for our own benefit.

Speaking
to God

SPEAKING TO GOD

How do I speak to God? In fact amongst those who follow the teachings and practices of Raja Yoga, we generally don't call Him 'God'. This term has the connotation of a great distance between Him and me. We see God, the Supreme Soul, as our Father and when talking with Him or of Him we use the term 'Baba' which is a very loving and intimate term for Father. With this term, Baba, we experience the feeling of a loving parent, the Father (and Mother) of the real me, the soul. He is truly my Father, my Spiritual Father, experientially.

I know very clearly that I make many mistakes. For example, I say many things I shouldn't. To break this habit, I develop the new habit of asking myself, in practical situations, what Baba would want me to say.

In asking Baba anything, it is important to understand that what He wants is never for His own benefit but always for my benefit. So if I am reacting to a situation with bitterness and resentment and instead of that I pause for a moment and ask Baba what He wants me to say, there can be no two answers; there must be respect, humility and gentleness. It is not that my response helps Him in any way but in doing as He wishes I am uplifted and I do not cause sorrow to others. This is what He wants. He has absolutely no personal motive of self-interest.

As I get to know Him, and learn to do what He wants, I become more and more like Him in my own thoughts and reactions and this is what He wants for me. Everything He wants is for my good.

An Experiment

An experiment

Here is a little experiment you might like to try. Take a piece of paper. Draw yourself as a little stick figure in the middle of the paper and then put around you all the personalities you have a close connection with. It may be wife or husband, a few friends, parents and other contacts such as doctor or lawyer. It could even be someone who is no longer physically around and yet still, in your mind, exerts an influence.

Notice the position each one is in, whether bigger or smaller, above or below you. Experiment with this little game. It will give you quite an insight into what is going on in your life. Having done that, put God on the map.

Where would God appear? Maybe on the level of acquaintance. Maybe I speak to

God once a week on Sunday, maybe twice a year at Christmas and Easter or maybe at those difficult times when there is no-one else; or maybe not at all. For me, I really know that I need God, that I cannot survive without that reliable Source of help, support and influence. Because I recognise my need, I bring God into the very centre of my life. It is when God is in this position that I enjoy His company and check with Him before I speak or act. A really major change takes place in my life on the basis of this relationship.

The Law of Karma

THE LAW OF KARMA

After knowing, or at least beginning to get to know, firstly myself and secondly God, the third step of spirituality is the understanding of the spiritual law of cause and effect. This is very much connected with knowledge of the self and the question of responsibility. To put it very simply, I am responsible for what is happening in my inner world and I am also responsible for what is happening in my external world. I have come to understand that this is the only way it can be. It cannot be God who is responsible. It cannot be anyone else, even though truly to accept that responsibility in my life brings a challenge at every single moment.

When I put the responsibility, whether for my inner self or external affairs 'out there' somewhere, then when all is going well I feel fine and the world is fine.   But when my contentment is derived from the outside world that is ever changing and over which I have little if any control I can so easily become unhappy and then I say it is because of this ... it is because of that ... or it is because of you that I am unhappy. But in Raja Yoga philosophy it is inaccurate to say that it is because of another person that I am unhappy.   I am responsible for my own feelings, emotions and even for my personality. I am responsible for the situation in which I find myself. This owning of full responsibility is not a sense of burden but is actually a sense of liberation. It means that I am not dependent on anything external or controlled by it. It means, for example, that I am not dependent on your bringing me flowers, making me a cup of tea or even giving me respect to make me happy. Rather, I know who I am and I am happy.

It means that I know in which direction my future is going because I am creating my own future. My future is within me. I have the responsibility but I also have the right. We love to think about our rights, but rights and responsibilities are two sides of the same coin.

It is spirituality which teaches me to see my responsibility and what causes I am setting in motion by my thoughts, words and actions. I just have to fulfil my responsibilities and the rights will automatically follow, because they are the effect. This may not happen immediately, but it is inevitable.

The law of cause and effect, action and reaction, or the law of karma is an integral part of spirituality. It gives us a basis on which to make right choices and create a beautiful future for ourselves and for the world around us.

Spiritual Progress

SPIRITUAL PROGRESS

The whole question of a relationship with God is a very personal one and the extent to which I want to allow this relationship to influence my life is entirely up to me. Many, many people have come to the Brahma Kumaris from all over the world and have heard at least some of these teachings. The basics of this knowledge can be learned in a course of seven or eight session offered free of charge at all centres.

Some of the people who complete this introduction say that they love the atmosphere at the centre, they enjoy Raja Yoga and want to continue coming occasionally for spiritual benefit. There are others who not only meditate and apply these principles in their lives but also see the importance of meditating and studying every day with a group of like-minded people and keeping that link with God throughout the day.

From this it can be seen that for some people meditation and spiritual study is significant but not a priority. For others, spirituality becomes their life's priority and they then take steps to adjust their lifestyle to help them achieve a deeper, clearer connection with God. To this end, we share the information we have as clearly and objectively as we can and leave each individual to decide how and to what extent he or she wants to use it.

About the author

B.K. Jayanti is a spiritual teacher and leader, a gifted meditator and an emissary for peace. She has a vision and experience that is truly global and deeply spiritual. Born in India of Sindhi parents, who migrated to England when she was eight years old, she is a blend of Eastern wisdom and Western education and culture.

At the age of 19 she embarked on a journey of spiritual study and service with the Brahma Kumaris World Spiritual University, and at the age of 21, decided to dedicate her life to this path. She has spent over 30 years in the company of some of the world's most remarkable yogis, gleaning much of their wisdom and insights. As a result, she herself is an extraordinary meditator and teacher and has developed a clarity and purity of mind that is exceptional.   B.K. Jayanti is also a much sought-after speaker around the world.

Her natural wisdom and gentle, though powerful, personality have touched and inspired hundreds of thousands of people. She is the European Director of the Brahma Kumaris World Spiritual University and assists in co-ordinating the University's activities in more than 70 countries.   She is also its main representative to the United Nations, Geneva.

ABOUT THE BRAHMA KUMARIS

The Brahma Kumaris World Spiritual University is an international organisation working at all levels of society for positive change. Established in 1937 it now carries out a wide range of educational programmes for the development of human and spiritual values throughout its 4000 centres in over 70 countries.

The University is a non-governmental organisation in general consultative status with the Economic and Social Council of the United Nations and in consultative status with UNICEF. It is also the recipient of seven UN Peace Messenger awards.

Locally, centres provide courses and lectures in meditation and positive values, enabling individuals to recognise their true potential and make the most of their lives. The University offers all its services free of charge.

INTERNATIONAL HEADQUARTERS

PO BOX No 2, MOUNT ABU, RAJASTHAN 307501, INDIA

Tel: (+91) 2974 38261-68   Fax: (+91) 2974 38952

E-mail: bkabu@vsnl.com

INTERNATIONAL CO-ORDINATING OFFICE & REGIONAL OFFICE FOR EUROPE AND THE MIDDLE EAST

Global Co-operation House, 65 Pound Lane, London, NW10 2HH, UK

Tel: (+44) 020 8727 3350 Fax: (+44) 020 8727 3351

E-mail: london@bkwsu.com

AFRICA

Global Museum for a Better World, Maua Close, off Parklands Road, Westlands, PO Box 12349, Nairobi, Kenya

Tel: (+254) 2 743 572   Fax: (+254) 2 743 885

E-mail: bkwsugm@holidaybazaar.com

AUSTRALIA AND EAST ASIA

78 Alt Street, Ashfield, Sydney, NSW 2131, Australia

Tel: (+61) 2 9716 7066   Fax: (+61) 2 9716 7795

E-mail: indra@one.net.au

NORTH AND SOUTH AMERICAS AND THE CARIBBEAN

Global Harmony House, 46 S. Middle Neck Road, Great Neck, NY 11021, USA
Tel: (+1) 516 773 0971   Fax: (+1) 516 773 0976
E-mail: newyork@bkwsu.com

RUSSIA AND CIS

Angels' House 2, Gospitalnaya Ploschad., Build 1, Moscow 111020, Russia
Tel: (+7) 095 263 02 47   Fax: (+7) 095 261 32 24
E-mail: bkwsu@mail.ru

www.bkwsu.com
www.bkpublications.com
e-mail enquiries@bkpublications.com